THE DISTANCE

★ BETWEEN ★

Your Dreams

&

Reality

IS CALLED

ACTION

Personal information

Name		
Home address	telephone	
	facsimile	

Company name		
Office address	telephone	
	facsimile	

Identification no.	
Driver's license no.	
Passport no.	

Blood group	Medic alert
Allergies	
Doctor	

In case of accident notify

Name		
Home address	telephone	
	facsimile	

Project Name										
Plan Start					Actual Start					
Plan Finish					Actual Finish					
Project Progress (%)	10	20	30	40	50	60	70	80	90	100
Completed date										
Note										

Project Name										
Plan Start					Actual Start					
Plan Finish					Actual Finish					
Project Progress (%)	10	20	30	40	50	60	70	80	90	100
Completed date										
Note										

Project Name										
Plan Start					Actual Start					
Plan Finish					Actual Finish					
Project Progress (%)	10	20	30	40	50	60	70	80	90	100
Completed date										
Note										

Project Name										
Plan Start					Actual Start					
Plan Finish					Actual Finish					
Project Progress (%)	10	20	30	40	50	60	70	80	90	100
Completed date										
Note										

Project Name										
Plan Start					Actual Start					
Plan Finish					Actual Finish					
Project Progress (%)	10	20	30	40	50	60	70	80	90	100
Completed date										
Note										

Business Goals

Project Name										
Plan Start					Actual Start					
Plan Finish					Actual Finish					
Project Progress (%)	10	20	30	40	50	60	70	80	90	100
Completed date										
Note										

Project Name										
Plan Start					Actual Start					
Plan Finish					Actual Finish					
Project Progress (%)	10	20	30	40	50	60	70	80	90	100
Completed date										
Note										

Project Name										
Plan Start					Actual Start					
Plan Finish					Actual Finish					
Project Progress (%)	10	20	30	40	50	60	70	80	90	100
Completed date										
Note										

Project Name										
Plan Start					Actual Start					
Plan Finish					Actual Finish					
Project Progress (%)	10	20	30	40	50	60	70	80	90	100
Completed date										
Note										

Project Name										
Plan Start					Actual Start					
Plan Finish					Actual Finish					
Project Progress (%)	10	20	30	40	50	60	70	80	90	100
Completed date										
Note										

Supplier Contact list

Supplier name	
Business	
Website	
Phone	
Email	
Note	

Supplier name	
Business	
Website	
Phone	
Email	
Note	

Supplier name	
Business	
Website	
Phone	
Email	
Note	

Supplier name	
Business	
Website	
Phone	
Email	
Note	

Supplier name	
Business	
Website	
Phone	
Email	
Note	

Supplier name	
Business	
Website	
Phone	
Email	
Note	

Supplier name	
Business	
Website	
Phone	
Email	
Note	

Supplier name	
Business	
Website	
Phone	
Email	
Note	

Supplier name	
Business	
Website	
Phone	
Email	
Note	

Supplier name	
Business	
Website	
Phone	
Email	
Note	

Supplier Contact list

Supplier name	
Business	
Website	
Phone	
Email	
Note	

Supplier name	
Business	
Website	
Phone	
Email	
Note	

Supplier name	
Business	
Website	
Phone	
Email	
Note	

Supplier name	
Business	
Website	
Phone	
Email	
Note	

Supplier name	
Business	
Website	
Phone	
Email	
Note	

Supplier name	
Business	
Website	
Phone	
Email	
Note	

Supplier name	
Business	
Website	
Phone	
Email	
Note	

Supplier name	
Business	
Website	
Phone	
Email	
Note	

Supplier name	
Business	
Website	
Phone	
Email	
Note	

Supplier name	
Business	
Website	
Phone	
Email	
Note	

Supplier Contact list

Supplier name	
Business	
Website	
Phone	
Email	
Note	

Supplier name	
Business	
Website	
Phone	
Email	
Note	

Supplier name	
Business	
Website	
Phone	
Email	
Note	

Supplier name	
Business	
Website	
Phone	
Email	
Note	

Supplier name	
Business	
Website	
Phone	
Email	
Note	

Supplier name	
Business	
Website	
Phone	
Email	
Note	

Supplier name	
Business	
Website	
Phone	
Email	
Note	

Supplier name	
Business	
Website	
Phone	
Email	
Note	

Supplier name	
Business	
Website	
Phone	
Email	
Note	

Supplier name	
Business	
Website	
Phone	
Email	
Note	

Supplier name	
Business	
Website	
Phone	
Email	
Note	

Supplier name	
Business	
Website	
Phone	
Email	
Note	

Supplier name	
Business	
Website	
Phone	
Email	
Note	

Supplier name	
Business	
Website	
Phone	
Email	
Note	

Supplier name	
Business	
Website	
Phone	
Email	
Note	

Supplier name	
Business	
Website	
Phone	
Email	
Note	

Supplier name	
Business	
Website	
Phone	
Email	
Note	

Supplier name	
Business	
Website	
Phone	
Email	
Note	

Supplier name	
Business	
Website	
Phone	
Email	
Note	

Supplier name	
Business	
Website	
Phone	
Email	
Note	

No.	Product	Item Description	Supplier	Website

	Vendors List			
No.	Product	Item Description	Supplier	Website

Vendors List				
No.	Product	Item Description	Supplier	Website

Vendors List				
No.	Product	Item Description	Supplier	Website

Vendors List				
No.	Product	Item Description	Supplier	Website

Vendors List				
No.	Product	Item Description	Supplier	Website

No.	Product	Description	Q'ty	Cost	Record date

Product Inventory

No.	Product	Description	Q'ty	Cost	Record date

Product Inventory

No.	Product	Description	Q'ty	Cost	Record date

No.	Product	Description	Q'ty	Cost	Record date

No.	Product	Description	Q'ty	Cost	Record date

	Product Inventory				
No.	Product	Description	Q'ty	Cost	Record date

Purchases & Sales				
No.	Product	Purchase Price	Sale Price	Profit

No.	Product	Purchase Price	Sale Price	Profit

Purchases & Sales				
No.	Product	Purchase Price	Sale Price	Profit

No.	Product	Purchase Price	Sale Price	Profit

No.	Product	Purchase Price	Sale Price	Profit

No.	Product	Purchase Price	Sale Price	Profit

Purchases & Sales

Order form

Order no.

Order Details

Date Ordered	
Date Shipped	
Tracking no.	
Shipped by	
Delivered by	
Date Received	

Customer Details

Customer name	
Company	
Address	
Phone	
Email	

No.	Item(s)	Q'ty	Unit Price	Discount	Total

Notes

Order no.

Order Details

Date Ordered	
Date Shipped	
Tracking no.	
Shipped by	
Delivered by	
Date Received	

Customer Details

Customer name	
Company	
Address	
Phone	
Email	

No.	Item(s)	Q'ty	Unit Price	Discount	Total

Notes

Order form

Order no.

Order Details			
ate Ordered			
ate Shipped			
acking no.			
hipped by			
elivered by			
ate Received			

Customer Details		
Customer name		
Company		
Address		
Phone		
Email		

lo.	Item(s)	Q'ty	Unit Price	Discount	Total

otes

Order no.

Order Details			
ate Ordered			
ate Shipped			
acking no.			
hipped by			
elivered by			
ate Received			

Customer Details		
Customer name		
Company		
Address		
Phone		
Email		

lo.	Item(s)	Q'ty	Unit Price	Discount	Total

otes

Order form

Order no.

Order Details

Date Ordered	
Date Shipped	
Tracking no.	
Shipped by	
Delivered by	
Date Received	

Customer Details

Customer name	
Company	
Address	
Phone	
Email	

No.	Item(s)	Q'ty	Unit Price	Discount	Total

Notes

Order no.

Order Details

Date Ordered	
Date Shipped	
Tracking no.	
Shipped by	
Delivered by	
Date Received	

Customer Details

Customer name	
Company	
Address	
Phone	
Email	

No.	Item(s)	Q'ty	Unit Price	Discount	Total

Notes

Order form

Order no.

Order Details

ate Ordered	
ate Shipped	
acking no.	
hipped by	
elivered by	
ate Received	

Customer Details

Customer name	
Company	
Address	
Phone	
Email	

No.	Item(s)	Q'ty	Unit Price	Discount	Total

otes

Order no.

Order Details

ate Ordered	
ate Shipped	
acking no.	
hipped by	
elivered by	
ate Received	

Customer Details

Customer name	
Company	
Address	
Phone	
Email	

No.	Item(s)	Q'ty	Unit Price	Discount	Total

otes

Order Information

Order form

Order no.

Order Details

Date Ordered	
Date Shipped	
Tracking no.	
Shipped by	
Delivered by	
Date Received	

Customer Details

Customer name	
Company	
Address	
Phone	
Email	

No.	Item(s)	Q'ty	Unit Price	Discount	Total

Notes

Order no.

Order Details

Date Ordered	
Date Shipped	
Tracking no.	
Shipped by	
Delivered by	
Date Received	

Customer Details

Customer name	
Company	
Address	
Phone	
Email	

No.	Item(s)	Q'ty	Unit Price	Discount	Total

Notes

Order form

Order no.

Order Details		Customer Details	
ate Ordered		Customer name	
ate Shipped		Company	
acking no.		Address	
hipped by			
elivered by		Phone	
ate Received		Email	

No.	Item(s)	Q'ty	Unit Price	Discount	Total

otes

Order no.

Order Details		Customer Details	
ate Ordered		Customer name	
ate Shipped		Company	
acking no.		Address	
hipped by			
elivered by		Phone	
ate Received		Email	

No.	Item(s)	Q'ty	Unit Price	Discount	Total

otes

Order form

Order no.

Order Details

Date Ordered	
Date Shipped	
Tracking no.	
Shipped by	
Delivered by	
Date Received	

Customer Details

Customer name	
Company	
Address	
Phone	
Email	

No.	Item(s)	Q'ty	Unit Price	Discount	Total

Notes

Order no.

Order Details

Date Ordered	
Date Shipped	
Tracking no.	
Shipped by	
Delivered by	
Date Received	

Customer Details

Customer name	
Company	
Address	
Phone	
Email	

No.	Item(s)	Q'ty	Unit Price	Discount	Total

Notes

Order form

Order no.

Order Details

ate Ordered	
ate Shipped	
acking no.	
hipped by	
elivered by	
ate Received	

Customer Details

Customer name	
Company	
Address	
Phone	
Email	

No.	Item(s)	Q'ty	Unit Price	Discount	Total

otes	

Order no.

Order Details

ate Ordered	
ate Shipped	
acking no.	
hipped by	
elivered by	
ate Received	

Customer Details

Customer name	
Company	
Address	
Phone	
Email	

No.	Item(s)	Q'ty	Unit Price	Discount	Total

otes	

Order form

Order no.

Order Details

Date Ordered	
Date Shipped	
Tracking no.	
Shipped by	
Delivered by	
Date Received	

Customer Details

Customer name	
Company	
Address	
Phone	
Email	

No.	Item(s)	Q'ty	Unit Price	Discount	Total

Notes

Order no.

Order Details

Date Ordered	
Date Shipped	
Tracking no.	
Shipped by	
Delivered by	
Date Received	

Customer Details

Customer name	
Company	
Address	
Phone	
Email	

No.	Item(s)	Q'ty	Unit Price	Discount	Total

Notes

Order form

Order no.

Order Details

ate Ordered	
ate Shipped	
acking no.	
ipped by	
elivered by	
ate Received	

Customer Details

Customer name	
Company	
Address	
Phone	
Email	

No.	Item(s)	Q'ty	Unit Price	Discount	Total

otes

Order no.

Order Details

ate Ordered	
ate Shipped	
acking no.	
ipped by	
elivered by	
ate Received	

Customer Details

Customer name	
Company	
Address	
Phone	
Email	

No.	Item(s)	Q'ty	Unit Price	Discount	Total

otes

Order form

Order no.

Order Details

Date Ordered	
Date Shipped	
Tracking no.	
Shipped by	
Delivered by	
Date Received	

Customer Details

Customer name	
Company	
Address	
Phone	
Email	

No.	Item(s)	Q'ty	Unit Price	Discount	Total

Notes

Order no.

Order Details

Date Ordered	
Date Shipped	
Tracking no.	
Shipped by	
Delivered by	
Date Received	

Customer Details

Customer name	
Company	
Address	
Phone	
Email	

No.	Item(s)	Q'ty	Unit Price	Discount	Total

Notes

Order form

Order no.

Order Details

Date Ordered	
Date Shipped	
Tracking no.	
Shipped by	
Delivered by	
Date Received	

Customer Details

Customer name	
Company	
Address	
Phone	
Email	

No.	Item(s)	Q'ty	Unit Price	Discount	Total

Notes

Order no.

Order Details

Date Ordered	
Date Shipped	
Tracking no.	
Shipped by	
Delivered by	
Date Received	

Customer Details

Customer name	
Company	
Address	
Phone	
Email	

No.	Item(s)	Q'ty	Unit Price	Discount	Total

Notes

Order form

Order no.

Order Details

Date Ordered	
Date Shipped	
Tracking no.	
Shipped by	
Delivered by	
Date Received	

Customer Details

Customer name	
Company	
Address	
Phone	
Email	

No.	Item(s)	Q'ty	Unit Price	Discount	Total

Notes

Order no.

Order Details

Date Ordered	
Date Shipped	
Tracking no.	
Shipped by	
Delivered by	
Date Received	

Customer Details

Customer name	
Company	
Address	
Phone	
Email	

No.	Item(s)	Q'ty	Unit Price	Discount	Total

Notes

Order form

Order no.

Order Details

ate Ordered	
ate Shipped	
acking no.	
hipped by	
elivered by	
ate Received	

Customer Details

Customer name	
Company	
Address	
Phone	
Email	

No.	Item(s)	Q'ty	Unit Price	Discount	Total

otes

Order no.

Order Details

ate Ordered	
ate Shipped	
acking no.	
hipped by	
elivered by	
ate Received	

Customer Details

Customer name	
Company	
Address	
Phone	
Email	

No.	Item(s)	Q'ty	Unit Price	Discount	Total

otes

Order form

Order no.

Order Details

Date Ordered	
Date Shipped	
Tracking no.	
Shipped by	
Delivered by	
Date Received	

Customer Details

Customer name	
Company	
Address	
Phone	
Email	

No.	Item(s)	Q'ty	Unit Price	Discount	Total

Notes

Order no.

Order Details

Date Ordered	
Date Shipped	
Tracking no.	
Shipped by	
Delivered by	
Date Received	

Customer Details

Customer name	
Company	
Address	
Phone	
Email	

No.	Item(s)	Q'ty	Unit Price	Discount	Total

Notes

Order form

Order no.

Order Details		Customer Details	
ate Ordered		Customer name	
ate Shipped		Company	
acking no.		Address	
ipped by			
elivered by		Phone	
ate Received		Email	

No.	Item(s)	Q'ty	Unit Price	Discount	Total

otes

Order no.

Order Details		Customer Details	
ate Ordered		Customer name	
ate Shipped		Company	
acking no.		Address	
ipped by			
elivered by		Phone	
ate Received		Email	

No.	Item(s)	Q'ty	Unit Price	Discount	Total

otes

Order form

Order no.

Order Details

Date Ordered	
Date Shipped	
Tracking no.	
Shipped by	
Delivered by	
Date Received	

Customer Details

Customer name	
Company	
Address	
Phone	
Email	

No.	Item(s)	Q'ty	Unit Price	Discount	Total

Notes

Order no.

Order Details

Date Ordered	
Date Shipped	
Tracking no.	
Shipped by	
Delivered by	
Date Received	

Customer Details

Customer name	
Company	
Address	
Phone	
Email	

No.	Item(s)	Q'ty	Unit Price	Discount	Total

Notes

Order form

Order no.

Order Details

Date Ordered	
Date Shipped	
Tracking no.	
Shipped by	
Delivered by	
Date Received	

Customer Details

Customer name	
Company	
Address	
Phone	
Email	

No.	Item(s)	Q'ty	Unit Price	Discount	Total

Notes

Order no.

Order Details

Date Ordered	
Date Shipped	
Tracking no.	
Shipped by	
Delivered by	
Date Received	

Customer Details

Customer name	
Company	
Address	
Phone	
Email	

No.	Item(s)	Q'ty	Unit Price	Discount	Total

Notes

Order form

Order no.

Order Details

Date Ordered	
Date Shipped	
Tracking no.	
Shipped by	
Delivered by	
Date Received	

Customer Details

Customer name	
Company	
Address	
Phone	
Email	

No.	Item(s)	Q'ty	Unit Price	Discount	Total

Notes

Order no.

Order Details

Date Ordered	
Date Shipped	
Tracking no.	
Shipped by	
Delivered by	
Date Received	

Customer Details

Customer name	
Company	
Address	
Phone	
Email	

No.	Item(s)	Q'ty	Unit Price	Discount	Total

Notes

Order form

Order no.

Order Details		Customer Details	
ate Ordered		Customer name	
ate Shipped		Company	
acking no.		Address	
ipped by			
elivered by		Phone	
ate Received		Email	

o.	Item(s)	Q'ty	Unit Price	Discount	Total

otes

Order no.

Order Details		Customer Details	
ate Ordered		Customer name	
ate Shipped		Company	
acking no.		Address	
ipped by			
elivered by		Phone	
ate Received		Email	

o.	Item(s)	Q'ty	Unit Price	Discount	Total

otes

Order form

Order no.

Order Details

Date Ordered	
Date Shipped	
Tracking no.	
Shipped by	
Delivered by	
Date Received	

Customer Details

Customer name	
Company	
Address	
Phone	
Email	

No.	Item(s)	Q'ty	Unit Price	Discount	Total

Notes

Order no.

Order Details

Date Ordered	
Date Shipped	
Tracking no.	
Shipped by	
Delivered by	
Date Received	

Customer Details

Customer name	
Company	
Address	
Phone	
Email	

No.	Item(s)	Q'ty	Unit Price	Discount	Total

Notes

Order form

Order no.

Order Details

ate Ordered	
ate Shipped	
acking no.	
hipped by	
elivered by	
ate Received	

Customer Details

Customer name	
Company	
Address	
Phone	
Email	

No.	Item(s)	Q'ty	Unit Price	Discount	Total

otes

Order no.

Order Details

ate Ordered	
ate Shipped	
acking no.	
hipped by	
elivered by	
ate Received	

Customer Details

Customer name	
Company	
Address	
Phone	
Email	

No.	Item(s)	Q'ty	Unit Price	Discount	Total

otes

Order form

Order no.

Order Details

Date Ordered	
Date Shipped	
Tracking no.	
Shipped by	
Delivered by	
Date Received	

Customer Details

Customer name	
Company	
Address	
Phone	
Email	

No.	Item(s)	Q'ty	Unit Price	Discount	Total

Notes

Order no.

Order Details

Date Ordered	
Date Shipped	
Tracking no.	
Shipped by	
Delivered by	
Date Received	

Customer Details

Customer name	
Company	
Address	
Phone	
Email	

No.	Item(s)	Q'ty	Unit Price	Discount	Total

Notes

Order form

Order no.

Order Details

ate Ordered	
ate Shipped	
acking no.	
hipped by	
elivered by	
ate Received	

Customer Details

Customer name	
Company	
Address	
Phone	
Email	

No.	Item(s)	Q'ty	Unit Price	Discount	Total

otes

Order no.

Order Details

ate Ordered	
ate Shipped	
acking no.	
hipped by	
elivered by	
ate Received	

Customer Details

Customer name	
Company	
Address	
Phone	
Email	

No.	Item(s)	Q'ty	Unit Price	Discount	Total

otes

Order form

Order no.

Order Details

Date Ordered	
Date Shipped	
Tracking no.	
Shipped by	
Delivered by	
Date Received	

Customer Details

Customer name	
Company	
Address	
Phone	
Email	

No.	Item(s)	Q'ty	Unit Price	Discount	Total

Notes

Order no.

Order Details

Date Ordered	
Date Shipped	
Tracking no.	
Shipped by	
Delivered by	
Date Received	

Customer Details

Customer name	
Company	
Address	
Phone	
Email	

No.	Item(s)	Q'ty	Unit Price	Discount	Total

Notes

Order form

Order no.

Order Details

ate Ordered	
ate Shipped	
cking no.	
ipped by	
elivered by	
ate Received	

Customer Details

Customer name	
Company	
Address	
Phone	
Email	

o.	Item(s)	Q'ty	Unit Price	Discount	Total

otes

Order no.

Order Details

ate Ordered	
ate Shipped	
cking no.	
ipped by	
elivered by	
ate Received	

Customer Details

Customer name	
Company	
Address	
Phone	
Email	

o.	Item(s)	Q'ty	Unit Price	Discount	Total

otes

Order form

Order no.

Order Details

Date Ordered	
Date Shipped	
Tracking no.	
Shipped by	
Delivered by	
Date Received	

Customer Details

Customer name	
Company	
Address	
Phone	
Email	

No.	Item(s)	Q'ty	Unit Price	Discount	Total

Notes

Order no.

Order Details

Date Ordered	
Date Shipped	
Tracking no.	
Shipped by	
Delivered by	
Date Received	

Customer Details

Customer name	
Company	
Address	
Phone	
Email	

No.	Item(s)	Q'ty	Unit Price	Discount	Total

Notes

Order form

Order no.

Order Details

ate Ordered	
ate Shipped	
acking no.	
hipped by	
elivered by	
ate Received	

Customer Details

Customer name	
Company	
Address	
Phone	
Email	

No.	Item(s)	Q'ty	Unit Price	Discount	Total

otes

Order no.

Order Details

ate Ordered	
ate Shipped	
acking no.	
hipped by	
elivered by	
ate Received	

Customer Details

Customer name	
Company	
Address	
Phone	
Email	

No.	Item(s)	Q'ty	Unit Price	Discount	Total

otes

Order form

Order no.

Order Details

Date Ordered	
Date Shipped	
Tracking no.	
Shipped by	
Delivered by	
Date Received	

Customer Details

Customer name	
Company	
Address	
Phone	
Email	

No.	Item(s)	Q'ty	Unit Price	Discount	Total

Notes

Order no.

Order Details

Date Ordered	
Date Shipped	
Tracking no.	
Shipped by	
Delivered by	
Date Received	

Customer Details

Customer name	
Company	
Address	
Phone	
Email	

No.	Item(s)	Q'ty	Unit Price	Discount	Total

Notes

Order form

Order no.

Order Details

ate Ordered	
ate Shipped	
acking no.	
nipped by	
elivered by	
ate Received	

Customer Details

Customer name	
Company	
Address	
Phone	
Email	

No.	Item(s)	Q'ty	Unit Price	Discount	Total

otes	

Order no.

Order Details

ate Ordered	
ate Shipped	
acking no.	
nipped by	
elivered by	
ate Received	

Customer Details

Customer name	
Company	
Address	
Phone	
Email	

No.	Item(s)	Q'ty	Unit Price	Discount	Total

otes	

Order form

Order no.

Order Details

Date Ordered	
Date Shipped	
Tracking no.	
Shipped by	
Delivered by	
Date Received	

Customer Details

Customer name	
Company	
Address	
Phone	
Email	

No.	Item(s)	Q'ty	Unit Price	Discount	Total

Notes

Order no.

Order Details

Date Ordered	
Date Shipped	
Tracking no.	
Shipped by	
Delivered by	
Date Received	

Customer Details

Customer name	
Company	
Address	
Phone	
Email	

No.	Item(s)	Q'ty	Unit Price	Discount	Total

Notes

Order form

Order no.

Order Details		Customer Details	
ate Ordered		Customer name	
ate Shipped		Company	
acking no.		Address	
ipped by			
elivered by		Phone	
ate Received		Email	

No.	Item(s)	Q'ty	Unit Price	Discount	Total

otes

Order no.

Order Details		Customer Details	
ate Ordered		Customer name	
ate Shipped		Company	
acking no.		Address	
ipped by			
elivered by		Phone	
ate Received		Email	

No.	Item(s)	Q'ty	Unit Price	Discount	Total

otes

Order form

Order no.

Order Details

Date Ordered	
Date Shipped	
Tracking no.	
Shipped by	
Delivered by	
Date Received	

Customer Details

Customer name	
Company	
Address	
Phone	
Email	

No.	Item(s)	Q'ty	Unit Price	Discount	Total

Notes

Order no.

Order Details

Date Ordered	
Date Shipped	
Tracking no.	
Shipped by	
Delivered by	
Date Received	

Customer Details

Customer name	
Company	
Address	
Phone	
Email	

No.	Item(s)	Q'ty	Unit Price	Discount	Total

Notes

Order form

Order no.

Order Details		Customer Details	
Date Ordered		Customer name	
Date Shipped		Company	
Tracking no.		Address	
Shipped by			
Delivered by		Phone	
Date Received		Email	

No.	Item(s)	Q'ty	Unit Price	Discount	Total

Notes

Order no.

Order Details		Customer Details	
Date Ordered		Customer name	
Date Shipped		Company	
Tracking no.		Address	
Shipped by			
Delivered by		Phone	
Date Received		Email	

No.	Item(s)	Q'ty	Unit Price	Discount	Total

Notes

Order form

Order no.

Order Details

Date Ordered	
Date Shipped	
Tracking no.	
Shipped by	
Delivered by	
Date Received	

Customer Details

Customer name	
Company	
Address	
Phone	
Email	

No.	Item(s)	Q'ty	Unit Price	Discount	Total

Notes

Order no.

Order Details

Date Ordered	
Date Shipped	
Tracking no.	
Shipped by	
Delivered by	
Date Received	

Customer Details

Customer name	
Company	
Address	
Phone	
Email	

No.	Item(s)	Q'ty	Unit Price	Discount	Total

Notes

Order form

Order no.

Order Details

Date Ordered	
Date Shipped	
Tracking no.	
Shipped by	
Delivered by	
Date Received	

Customer Details

Customer name	
Company	
Address	
Phone	
Email	

No.	Item(s)	Q'ty	Unit Price	Discount	Total

Notes

Order no.

Order Details

Date Ordered	
Date Shipped	
Tracking no.	
Shipped by	
Delivered by	
Date Received	

Customer Details

Customer name	
Company	
Address	
Phone	
Email	

No.	Item(s)	Q'ty	Unit Price	Discount	Total

Notes

Order form

Order no.

Order Details

Date Ordered	
Date Shipped	
Tracking no.	
Shipped by	
Delivered by	
Date Received	

Customer Details

Customer name	
Company	
Address	
Phone	
Email	

No.	Item(s)	Q'ty	Unit Price	Discount	Total

Notes

Order no.

Order Details

Date Ordered	
Date Shipped	
Tracking no.	
Shipped by	
Delivered by	
Date Received	

Customer Details

Customer name	
Company	
Address	
Phone	
Email	

No.	Item(s)	Q'ty	Unit Price	Discount	Total

Notes

Order form

Order no.

Order Details

ate Ordered	
ate Shipped	
acking no.	
hipped by	
elivered by	
ate Received	

Customer Details

Customer name	
Company	
Address	
Phone	
Email	

No.	Item(s)	Q'ty	Unit Price	Discount	Total

otes

Order no.

Order Details

ate Ordered	
ate Shipped	
acking no.	
ipped by	
elivered by	
ate Received	

Customer Details

Customer name	
Company	
Address	
Phone	
Email	

No.	Item(s)	Q'ty	Unit Price	Discount	Total

otes

Order form

Order no.

Order Details

Date Ordered	
Date Shipped	
Tracking no.	
Shipped by	
Delivered by	
Date Received	

Customer Details

Customer name	
Company	
Address	
Phone	
Email	

No.	Item(s)	Q'ty	Unit Price	Discount	Total

Notes

Order no.

Order Details

Date Ordered	
Date Shipped	
Tracking no.	
Shipped by	
Delivered by	
Date Received	

Customer Details

Customer name	
Company	
Address	
Phone	
Email	

No.	Item(s)	Q'ty	Unit Price	Discount	Total

Notes

Order form

Order no.

Order Details

ate Ordered	
ate Shipped	
acking no.	
hipped by	
elivered by	
ate Received	

Customer Details

Customer name	
Company	
Address	
Phone	
Email	

No.	Item(s)	Q'ty	Unit Price	Discount	Total

otes

Order no.

Order Details

ate Ordered	
ate Shipped	
acking no.	
hipped by	
elivered by	
ate Received	

Customer Details

Customer name	
Company	
Address	
Phone	
Email	

No.	Item(s)	Q'ty	Unit Price	Discount	Total

otes

Order form

Order no.

Order Details

Date Ordered	
Date Shipped	
Tracking no.	
Shipped by	
Delivered by	
Date Received	

Customer Details

Customer name	
Company	
Address	
Phone	
Email	

No.	Item(s)	Q'ty	Unit Price	Discount	Total

Notes

Order no.

Order Details

Date Ordered	
Date Shipped	
Tracking no.	
Shipped by	
Delivered by	
Date Received	

Customer Details

Customer name	
Company	
Address	
Phone	
Email	

No.	Item(s)	Q'ty	Unit Price	Discount	Total

Notes

Order form

Order no.

Order Details

Date Ordered	
Date Shipped	
Tracking no.	
Shipped by	
Delivered by	
Date Received	

Customer Details

Customer name	
Company	
Address	
Phone	
Email	

No.	Item(s)	Q'ty	Unit Price	Discount	Total

Notes

Order no.

Order Details

Date Ordered	
Date Shipped	
Tracking no.	
Shipped by	
Delivered by	
Date Received	

Customer Details

Customer name	
Company	
Address	
Phone	
Email	

No.	Item(s)	Q'ty	Unit Price	Discount	Total

Notes

Order form

Order no.

Order Details

Date Ordered	
Date Shipped	
Tracking no.	
Shipped by	
Delivered by	
Date Received	

Customer Details

Customer name	
Company	
Address	
Phone	
Email	

No.	Item(s)	Q'ty	Unit Price	Discount	Total

Notes

Order no.

Order Details

Date Ordered	
Date Shipped	
Tracking no.	
Shipped by	
Delivered by	
Date Received	

Customer Details

Customer name	
Company	
Address	
Phone	
Email	

No.	Item(s)	Q'ty	Unit Price	Discount	Total

Notes

Order form

Order no.

Order Details

Date Ordered	
Date Shipped	
Tracking no.	
Shipped by	
Delivered by	
Date Received	

Customer Details

Customer name	
Company	
Address	
Phone	
Email	

No.	Item(s)	Q'ty	Unit Price	Discount	Total

Notes

Order no.

Order Details

Date Ordered	
Date Shipped	
Tracking no.	
Shipped by	
Delivered by	
Date Received	

Customer Details

Customer name	
Company	
Address	
Phone	
Email	

No.	Item(s)	Q'ty	Unit Price	Discount	Total

Notes

Order form

Order no.

Order Details		Customer Details	
Date Ordered		Customer name	
Date Shipped		Company	
Tracking no.		Address	
Shipped by			
Delivered by		Phone	
Date Received		Email	

No.	Item(s)	Q'ty	Unit Price	Discount	Total

Notes

Order no.

Order Details		Customer Details	
Date Ordered		Customer name	
Date Shipped		Company	
Tracking no.		Address	
Shipped by			
Delivered by		Phone	
Date Received		Email	

No.	Item(s)	Q'ty	Unit Price	Discount	Total

Notes

Order form

Order no.

Order Details

ate Ordered	
ate Shipped	
acking no.	
hipped by	
elivered by	
ate Received	

Customer Details

Customer name	
Company	
Address	
Phone	
Email	

No.	Item(s)	Q'ty	Unit Price	Discount	Total

otes

Order no.

Order Details

ate Ordered	
ate Shipped	
acking no.	
ipped by	
elivered by	
ate Received	

Customer Details

Customer name	
Company	
Address	
Phone	
Email	

No.	Item(s)	Q'ty	Unit Price	Discount	Total

otes

Order Information

Order form

Order no.

Order Details

Date Ordered	
Date Shipped	
Tracking no.	
Shipped by	
Delivered by	
Date Received	

Customer Details

Customer name	
Company	
Address	
Phone	
Email	

No.	Item(s)	Q'ty	Unit Price	Discount	Total

Notes

Order no.

Order Details

Date Ordered	
Date Shipped	
Tracking no.	
Shipped by	
Delivered by	
Date Received	

Customer Details

Customer name	
Company	
Address	
Phone	
Email	

No.	Item(s)	Q'ty	Unit Price	Discount	Total

Notes

Order form

Order no.

Order Details

Date Ordered	
Date Shipped	
Tracking no.	
Shipped by	
Delivered by	
Date Received	

Customer Details

Customer name	
Company	
Address	
Phone	
Email	

No.	Item(s)	Q'ty	Unit Price	Discount	Total

Notes

Order no.

Order Details

Date Ordered	
Date Shipped	
Tracking no.	
Shipped by	
Delivered by	
Date Received	

Customer Details

Customer name	
Company	
Address	
Phone	
Email	

No.	Item(s)	Q'ty	Unit Price	Discount	Total

Notes

Order form

Order no.

Order Details

Date Ordered	
Date Shipped	
Tracking no.	
Shipped by	
Delivered by	
Date Received	

Customer Details

Customer name	
Company	
Address	
Phone	
Email	

No.	Item(s)	Q'ty	Unit Price	Discount	Total

Notes

Order no.

Order Details

Date Ordered	
Date Shipped	
Tracking no.	
Shipped by	
Delivered by	
Date Received	

Customer Details

Customer name	
Company	
Address	
Phone	
Email	

No.	Item(s)	Q'ty	Unit Price	Discount	Total

Notes

Order form

Order no.

Order Details

Date Ordered	
Date Shipped	
Tracking no.	
Shipped by	
Delivered by	
Date Received	

Customer Details

Customer name	
Company	
Address	
Phone	
Email	

No.	Item(s)	Q'ty	Unit Price	Discount	Total

Notes

Order no.

Order Details

Date Ordered	
Date Shipped	
Tracking no.	
Shipped by	
Delivered by	
Date Received	

Customer Details

Customer name	
Company	
Address	
Phone	
Email	

No.	Item(s)	Q'ty	Unit Price	Discount	Total

Notes

Order form

Order no.

Order Details

Date Ordered	
Date Shipped	
Tracking no.	
Shipped by	
Delivered by	
Date Received	

Customer Details

Customer name	
Company	
Address	
Phone	
Email	

No.	Item(s)	Q'ty	Unit Price	Discount	Total

Notes

Order no.

Order Details

Date Ordered	
Date Shipped	
Tracking no.	
Shipped by	
Delivered by	
Date Received	

Customer Details

Customer name	
Company	
Address	
Phone	
Email	

No.	Item(s)	Q'ty	Unit Price	Discount	Total

Notes

Order form

Order no.

Order Details

Date Ordered	
Date Shipped	
Tracking no.	
Shipped by	
Delivered by	
Date Received	

Customer Details

Customer name	
Company	
Address	
Phone	
Email	

No.	Item(s)	Q'ty	Unit Price	Discount	Total

Notes

Order no.

Order Details

Date Ordered	
Date Shipped	
Tracking no.	
Shipped by	
Delivered by	
Date Received	

Customer Details

Customer name	
Company	
Address	
Phone	
Email	

No.	Item(s)	Q'ty	Unit Price	Discount	Total

Notes

Order form

Order no.

Order Details

Date Ordered	
Date Shipped	
Tracking no.	
Shipped by	
Delivered by	
Date Received	

Customer Details

Customer name	
Company	
Address	
Phone	
Email	

No.	Item(s)	Q'ty	Unit Price	Discount	Total

Notes

Order no.

Order Details

Date Ordered	
Date Shipped	
Tracking no.	
Shipped by	
Delivered by	
Date Received	

Customer Details

Customer name	
Company	
Address	
Phone	
Email	

No.	Item(s)	Q'ty	Unit Price	Discount	Total

Notes

Order form

Order no.

Order Details

ate Ordered	
ate Shipped	
acking no.	
hipped by	
elivered by	
ate Received	

Customer Details

Customer name	
Company	
Address	
Phone	
Email	

No.	Item(s)	Q'ty	Unit Price	Discount	Total

otes

Order no.

Order Details

ate Ordered	
ate Shipped	
acking no.	
hipped by	
elivered by	
ate Received	

Customer Details

Customer name	
Company	
Address	
Phone	
Email	

No.	Item(s)	Q'ty	Unit Price	Discount	Total

otes

Order form

Order no.

Order Details

Date Ordered	
Date Shipped	
Tracking no.	
Shipped by	
Delivered by	
Date Received	

Customer Details

Customer name	
Company	
Address	
Phone	
Email	

No.	Item(s)	Q'ty	Unit Price	Discount	Total

Notes

Order no.

Order Details

Date Ordered	
Date Shipped	
Tracking no.	
Shipped by	
Delivered by	
Date Received	

Customer Details

Customer name	
Company	
Address	
Phone	
Email	

No.	Item(s)	Q'ty	Unit Price	Discount	Total

Notes

Order form

Order no.

Order Details	
ate Ordered	
ate Shipped	
acking no.	
hipped by	
elivered by	
ate Received	

Customer Details	
Customer name	
Company	
Address	
Phone	
Email	

No.	Item(s)	Q'ty	Unit Price	Discount	Total

otes

Order no.

Order Details	
ate Ordered	
ate Shipped	
acking no.	
hipped by	
elivered by	
ate Received	

Customer Details	
Customer name	
Company	
Address	
Phone	
Email	

No.	Item(s)	Q'ty	Unit Price	Discount	Total

otes

Order form

Order no.

Order Details

Date Ordered	
Date Shipped	
Tracking no.	
Shipped by	
Delivered by	
Date Received	

Customer Details

Customer name	
Company	
Address	
Phone	
Email	

No.	Item(s)	Q'ty	Unit Price	Discount	Total

Notes

Order no.

Order Details

Date Ordered	
Date Shipped	
Tracking no.	
Shipped by	
Delivered by	
Date Received	

Customer Details

Customer name	
Company	
Address	
Phone	
Email	

No.	Item(s)	Q'ty	Unit Price	Discount	Total

Notes

Order form

Order no.

Order Details

Date Ordered	
Date Shipped	
Tracking no.	
Shipped by	
Delivered by	
Date Received	

Customer Details

Customer name	
Company	
Address	
Phone	
Email	

No.	Item(s)	Q'ty	Unit Price	Discount	Total

Notes

Order no.

Order Details

Date Ordered	
Date Shipped	
Tracking no.	
Shipped by	
Delivered by	
Date Received	

Customer Details

Customer name	
Company	
Address	
Phone	
Email	

No.	Item(s)	Q'ty	Unit Price	Discount	Total

Notes

Order Information

Order form

Order no.

Order Details

Date Ordered	
Date Shipped	
Tracking no.	
Shipped by	
Delivered by	
Date Received	

Customer Details

Customer name	
Company	
Address	
Phone	
Email	

No.	Item(s)	Q'ty	Unit Price	Discount	Total

Notes

Order no.

Order Details

Date Ordered	
Date Shipped	
Tracking no.	
Shipped by	
Delivered by	
Date Received	

Customer Details

Customer name	
Company	
Address	
Phone	
Email	

No.	Item(s)	Q'ty	Unit Price	Discount	Total

Notes

Order form

Order no.

Order Details		Customer Details	
ate Ordered		Customer name	
ate Shipped		Company	
acking no.		Address	
hipped by			
elivered by		Phone	
ate Received		Email	

No.	Item(s)	Q'ty	Unit Price	Discount	Total

otes

Order no.

Order Details		Customer Details	
ate Ordered		Customer name	
ate Shipped		Company	
acking no.		Address	
ipped by			
elivered by		Phone	
ate Received		Email	

No.	Item(s)	Q'ty	Unit Price	Discount	Total

otes

Order form

Order no.

Order Details

Date Ordered	
Date Shipped	
Tracking no.	
Shipped by	
Delivered by	
Date Received	

Customer Details

Customer name	
Company	
Address	
Phone	
Email	

No.	Item(s)	Q'ty	Unit Price	Discount	Total

Notes

Order no.

Order Details

Date Ordered	
Date Shipped	
Tracking no.	
Shipped by	
Delivered by	
Date Received	

Customer Details

Customer name	
Company	
Address	
Phone	
Email	

No.	Item(s)	Q'ty	Unit Price	Discount	Total

Notes

Order form

Order no.

Order Details		Customer Details	
ate Ordered		Customer name	
ate Shipped		Company	
acking no.		Address	
nipped by			
elivered by		Phone	
ate Received		Email	

No.	Item(s)	Q'ty	Unit Price	Discount	Total

otes

Order no.

Order Details		Customer Details	
ate Ordered		Customer name	
ate Shipped		Company	
acking no.		Address	
nipped by			
elivered by		Phone	
ate Received		Email	

No.	Item(s)	Q'ty	Unit Price	Discount	Total

otes

Order form

Order no.

Order Details

Date Ordered	
Date Shipped	
Tracking no.	
Shipped by	
Delivered by	
Date Received	

Customer Details

Customer name	
Company	
Address	
Phone	
Email	

No.	Item(s)	Q'ty	Unit Price	Discount	Total

Notes

Order no.

Order Details

Date Ordered	
Date Shipped	
Tracking no.	
Shipped by	
Delivered by	
Date Received	

Customer Details

Customer name	
Company	
Address	
Phone	
Email	

No.	Item(s)	Q'ty	Unit Price	Discount	Total

Notes

Order form

Order no.

Order Details

ate Ordered	
ate Shipped	
acking no.	
hipped by	
elivered by	
ate Received	

Customer Details

Customer name	
Company	
Address	
Phone	
Email	

No.	Item(s)	Q'ty	Unit Price	Discount	Total

otes

Order no.

Order Details

ate Ordered	
ate Shipped	
acking no.	
hipped by	
elivered by	
ate Received	

Customer Details

Customer name	
Company	
Address	
Phone	
Email	

No.	Item(s)	Q'ty	Unit Price	Discount	Total

otes

Order form

Order no.

Order Details

Date Ordered	
Date Shipped	
Tracking no.	
Shipped by	
Delivered by	
Date Received	

Customer Details

Customer name	
Company	
Address	
Phone	
Email	

No.	Item(s)	Q'ty	Unit Price	Discount	Total

Notes

Order no.

Order Details

Date Ordered	
Date Shipped	
Tracking no.	
Shipped by	
Delivered by	
Date Received	

Customer Details

Customer name	
Company	
Address	
Phone	
Email	

No.	Item(s)	Q'ty	Unit Price	Discount	Total

Notes

Order form

Order no.

Order Details	
ate Ordered	
ate Shipped	
acking no.	
hipped by	
elivered by	
ate Received	

Customer Details	
Customer name	
Company	
Address	
Phone	
Email	

No.	Item(s)	Q'ty	Unit Price	Discount	Total

otes

Order no.

Order Details	
ate Ordered	
ate Shipped	
acking no.	
hipped by	
elivered by	
ate Received	

Customer Details	
Customer name	
Company	
Address	
Phone	
Email	

No.	Item(s)	Q'ty	Unit Price	Discount	Total

otes

Order form

Order no.

Order Details

Date Ordered	
Date Shipped	
Tracking no.	
Shipped by	
Delivered by	
Date Received	

Customer Details

Customer name	
Company	
Address	
Phone	
Email	

No.	Item(s)	Q'ty	Unit Price	Discount	Total

Notes

Order no.

Order Details

Date Ordered	
Date Shipped	
Tracking no.	
Shipped by	
Delivered by	
Date Received	

Customer Details

Customer name	
Company	
Address	
Phone	
Email	

No.	Item(s)	Q'ty	Unit Price	Discount	Total

Notes

Order form

Order no.

Order Details

ate Ordered	
ate Shipped	
acking no.	
hipped by	
elivered by	
ate Received	

Customer Details

Customer name	
Company	
Address	
Phone	
Email	

No.	Item(s)	Q'ty	Unit Price	Discount	Total

otes

Order no.

Order Details

ate Ordered	
ate Shipped	
acking no.	
hipped by	
elivered by	
ate Received	

Customer Details

Customer name	
Company	
Address	
Phone	
Email	

No.	Item(s)	Q'ty	Unit Price	Discount	Total

otes

Order form

Order no.

Order Details

Date Ordered	
Date Shipped	
Tracking no.	
Shipped by	
Delivered by	
Date Received	

Customer Details

Customer name	
Company	
Address	
Phone	
Email	

No.	Item(s)	Q'ty	Unit Price	Discount	Total

Notes

Order no.

Order Details

Date Ordered	
Date Shipped	
Tracking no.	
Shipped by	
Delivered by	
Date Received	

Customer Details

Customer name	
Company	
Address	
Phone	
Email	

No.	Item(s)	Q'ty	Unit Price	Discount	Total

Notes

Order form

Order no.

Order Details

ate Ordered	
ate Shipped	
acking no.	
hipped by	
elivered by	
ate Received	

Customer Details

Customer name	
Company	
Address	
Phone	
Email	

No.	Item(s)	Q'ty	Unit Price	Discount	Total

otes

Order no.

Order Details

ate Ordered	
ate Shipped	
acking no.	
ipped by	
elivered by	
ate Received	

Customer Details

Customer name	
Company	
Address	
Phone	
Email	

No.	Item(s)	Q'ty	Unit Price	Discount	Total

otes

Order form

Order no.

Order Details

Date Ordered	
Date Shipped	
Tracking no.	
Shipped by	
Delivered by	
Date Received	

Customer Details

Customer name	
Company	
Address	
Phone	
Email	

No.	Item(s)	Q'ty	Unit Price	Discount	Total

Notes

Order no.

Order Details

Date Ordered	
Date Shipped	
Tracking no.	
Shipped by	
Delivered by	
Date Received	

Customer Details

Customer name	
Company	
Address	
Phone	
Email	

No.	Item(s)	Q'ty	Unit Price	Discount	Total

Notes

Order form

Order no.

Order Details

ate Ordered	
ate Shipped	
acking no.	
nipped by	
elivered by	
ate Received	

Customer Details

Customer name	
Company	
Address	
Phone	
Email	

No.	Item(s)	Q'ty	Unit Price	Discount	Total

otes

Order no.

Order Details

ate Ordered	
ate Shipped	
acking no.	
nipped by	
elivered by	
ate Received	

Customer Details

Customer name	
Company	
Address	
Phone	
Email	

No.	Item(s)	Q'ty	Unit Price	Discount	Total

otes

Order Information

Order form

Order no.

Order Details

Date Ordered	
Date Shipped	
Tracking no.	
Shipped by	
Delivered by	
Date Received	

Customer Details

Customer name	
Company	
Address	
Phone	
Email	

No.	Item(s)	Q'ty	Unit Price	Discount	Total

Notes

Order no.

Order Details

Date Ordered	
Date Shipped	
Tracking no.	
Shipped by	
Delivered by	
Date Received	

Customer Details

Customer name	
Company	
Address	
Phone	
Email	

No.	Item(s)	Q'ty	Unit Price	Discount	Total

Notes

Order form

Order no.

Order Details

Date Ordered	
Date Shipped	
Tracking no.	
Shipped by	
Delivered by	
Date Received	

Customer Details

Customer name	
Company	
Address	
Phone	
Email	

No.	Item(s)	Q'ty	Unit Price	Discount	Total

Notes

Order no.

Order Details

Date Ordered	
Date Shipped	
Tracking no.	
Shipped by	
Delivered by	
Date Received	

Customer Details

Customer name	
Company	
Address	
Phone	
Email	

No.	Item(s)	Q'ty	Unit Price	Discount	Total

Notes

Order form

Order no.

Order Details

Date Ordered	
Date Shipped	
Tracking no.	
Shipped by	
Delivered by	
Date Received	

Customer Details

Customer name	
Company	
Address	
Phone	
Email	

No.	Item(s)	Q'ty	Unit Price	Discount	Total

Notes

Order no.

Order Details

Date Ordered	
Date Shipped	
Tracking no.	
Shipped by	
Delivered by	
Date Received	

Customer Details

Customer name	
Company	
Address	
Phone	
Email	

No.	Item(s)	Q'ty	Unit Price	Discount	Total

Notes

Order form

Order no.

Order Details		Customer Details	
ate Ordered		Customer name	
ate Shipped		Company	
acking no.		Address	
hipped by			
elivered by		Phone	
ate Received		Email	

No.	Item(s)	Q'ty	Unit Price	Discount	Total

otes

Order no.

Order Details		Customer Details	
ate Ordered		Customer name	
ate Shipped		Company	
acking no.		Address	
hipped by			
elivered by		Phone	
ate Received		Email	

No.	Item(s)	Q'ty	Unit Price	Discount	Total

otes

Order form

Order no.

Order Details

Date Ordered	
Date Shipped	
Tracking no.	
Shipped by	
Delivered by	
Date Received	

Customer Details

Customer name	
Company	
Address	
Phone	
Email	

No.	Item(s)	Q'ty	Unit Price	Discount	Total

Notes

Order no.

Order Details

Date Ordered	
Date Shipped	
Tracking no.	
Shipped by	
Delivered by	
Date Received	

Customer Details

Customer name	
Company	
Address	
Phone	
Email	

No.	Item(s)	Q'ty	Unit Price	Discount	Total

Notes

Order form

Order no.

Order Details		Customer Details	
ate Ordered		Customer name	
ate Shipped		Company	
acking no.		Address	
hipped by			
elivered by		Phone	
ate Received		Email	

No.	Item(s)	Q'ty	Unit Price	Discount	Total

otes

Order no.

Order Details		Customer Details	
ate Ordered		Customer name	
ate Shipped		Company	
acking no.		Address	
hipped by			
elivered by		Phone	
ate Received		Email	

No.	Item(s)	Q'ty	Unit Price	Discount	Total

otes

Order form

Order no.

Order Details

Date Ordered	
Date Shipped	
Tracking no.	
Shipped by	
Delivered by	
Date Received	

Customer Details

Customer name	
Company	
Address	
Phone	
Email	

No.	Item(s)	Q'ty	Unit Price	Discount	Total

Notes

Order no.

Order Details

Date Ordered	
Date Shipped	
Tracking no.	
Shipped by	
Delivered by	
Date Received	

Customer Details

Customer name	
Company	
Address	
Phone	
Email	

No.	Item(s)	Q'ty	Unit Price	Discount	Total

Notes

Order form

Order no.

<table>
<tr><td colspan="2">Order Details</td><td colspan="2">Customer Details</td></tr>
<tr><td>ate Ordered</td><td></td><td>Customer name</td><td></td></tr>
<tr><td>ate Shipped</td><td></td><td>Company</td><td></td></tr>
<tr><td>acking no.</td><td></td><td>Address</td><td></td></tr>
<tr><td>hipped by</td><td></td><td></td><td></td></tr>
<tr><td>elivered by</td><td></td><td>Phone</td><td></td></tr>
<tr><td>ate Received</td><td></td><td>Email</td><td></td></tr>
</table>

No.	Item(s)	Q'ty	Unit Price	Discount	Total

otes

Order no.

<table>
<tr><td colspan="2">Order Details</td><td colspan="2">Customer Details</td></tr>
<tr><td>ate Ordered</td><td></td><td>Customer name</td><td></td></tr>
<tr><td>ate Shipped</td><td></td><td>Company</td><td></td></tr>
<tr><td>acking no.</td><td></td><td>Address</td><td></td></tr>
<tr><td>hipped by</td><td></td><td></td><td></td></tr>
<tr><td>elivered by</td><td></td><td>Phone</td><td></td></tr>
<tr><td>ate Received</td><td></td><td>Email</td><td></td></tr>
</table>

No.	Item(s)	Q'ty	Unit Price	Discount	Total

otes

Order form

Order no.

Order Details

Date Ordered	
Date Shipped	
Tracking no.	
Shipped by	
Delivered by	
Date Received	

Customer Details

Customer name	
Company	
Address	
Phone	
Email	

No.	Item(s)	Q'ty	Unit Price	Discount	Total

Notes

Order no.

Order Details

Date Ordered	
Date Shipped	
Tracking no.	
Shipped by	
Delivered by	
Date Received	

Customer Details

Customer name	
Company	
Address	
Phone	
Email	

No.	Item(s)	Q'ty	Unit Price	Discount	Total

Notes

Order form

Order no.

Order Details

Date Ordered	
Date Shipped	
Tracking no.	
Shipped by	
Delivered by	
Date Received	

Customer Details

Customer name	
Company	
Address	
Phone	
Email	

No.	Item(s)	Q'ty	Unit Price	Discount	Total

Notes

Order no.

Order Details

Date Ordered	
Date Shipped	
Tracking no.	
Shipped by	
Delivered by	
Date Received	

Customer Details

Customer name	
Company	
Address	
Phone	
Email	

No.	Item(s)	Q'ty	Unit Price	Discount	Total

Notes

No.	Refer order no.	Items	Q'ty	Note

Information of Returns items

No.	Refer order no.	Items	Q'ty	Note

Information of Returns items

Monthly Sales			
Month	Total Units	Sale Price	Profit
January			
	note		
February			
	note		
March			
	note		
April			
	note		
May			
	note		
June			
	note		
July			
	note		
August			
	note		
September			
	note		
October			
	note		
November			
	note		
December			
	note		

Month	Income	Expenses	Balance
January			
	note		
February			
	note		
March			
	note		
April			
	note		
May			
	note		
June			
	note		
July			
	note		
August			
	note		
September			
	note		
October			
	note		
November			
	note		
December			
	note		

Made in the USA
Monee, IL
30 June 2021